The
Newest
and
Coolest
Dinosaurs

By Philip J. Currie and Colleayn O. Mastin
Illustrations by Jan Sovak

Irritator
The Irritating Dinosaur

Have you ever been irritated because you could not correctly put together a puzzle? Even though you had all the pieces? Well, that is exactly what happened to the scientists working on Irritator—that irritating dinosaur! Scientists had a hard time identifying this dinosaur. For one thing, collectors of dinosaur fossils had not properly put together the front of the skull of the only known specimen.

For another, the creature had been discovered in marine sediments in South America. Dinosaurs lived on land, but occasionally when one died, its body was light enough to be carried by river currents far out to sea. That happened to the Irritator specimen and caused additional problems in identifying the beast.

Finally, someone realized that the long-snouted Irritator that was found in marine rocks from Brazil was probably the traveling kind, in death if not in life. Leaving behind its probable relatives, Baryonyx from England and Spinosaurus from Morocco, it ended up in Brazil. These three animals had long, low skulls and looked more like crocodiles than their closer relative, Tyrannosaurus rex. They may, in fact, have mimicked crocodiles.

A dentist's dream, Irritator had lots of teeth in its crocodile-like mouth. But rather than going to a dentist for regular teeth cleanings, Irritator regularly replaced its teeth by growing new ones.

Irritator lived during the Early Cretaceous period. This was the time when the surface of the earth was slowly breaking up into smaller parcels of land and dinosaurs disappeared from this planet.

Dino Data

Name	Irritator
Means	Irritating
Year described	1996
Food	fish
Family	Sinosauridae (Theropoda)
Lived	Early Cretaceous
Fossils	Brazil
Length	5 meters (16 feet)
Weight	2 metric tons (4,400 pounds)

In the heat of the afternoon, a fishing-eating Irritator takes to the shade. Later, it will return to the river to feed on fish.

Sinosauropteryx
The First Feathered Dinosaur

In 1996 this remarkable small feathered dinosaur was discovered in northeastern China. However, if you were a small mammal or lizard, chances are you would not have cared about its size. You would have been too busy trying to set new speed records escaping its jaws.

It is rare to find small dinosaurs, so the discovery of a completely preserved, turkey-sized skeleton was amazing enough to be very important. But what shocked the dino detectives were the featherlike impressions in the rock around the boundary of the specimen.

The presence of this insulating layer of simple featherlike structures (called protofeathers) also suggests that this dinosaur may have been warm blooded. These protofeathers were not used for flight, but probably to keep this small, meat-eating dinosaur warm. It will take several years before it can be determined with certainty whether these are real feathers like those of birds.

Two more skeletons of Sinosauropteryx have been found in China. Both were found with fossilized stomach contents that clearly show the dinosaur was hunting, killing and eating both lizards and mammals. One mother Sinosauropteryx had two eggs inside her body, which show that Sinosauropteryx had babies by laying eggs.

Dino Data

Name	Sinosauropteryx
Name means	Chinese reptile feather
Year describe	1996
Food	lizards and mammals
Family	Compognathidae (Theropoda)
Lived	Early Cretaceous
Fossils	Liaoning, China
Length	1.5 meters (5 feet)
Weight	10 kilograms (22 pounds)

A **Sinosauropteryx** mother hides her eggs in dense vegetation. She knows large carnivores and the other hungry creatures lurk in the nearby forest. Keeping a close watch on her nest is important. She must be careful.

Andesaurus

This towering long-necked sauropod lived in South America in the Early to Late Cretaceous period over 100 million years ago.

Herds of these huge plant-eaters may have roamed through the vast green forests of South America, stretching their long necks high into the trees to find food.

This large sauropod was about the length of a semi-trailer truck unit. The distance from its hip bone to the ground was about twice the height of a tall man. Long-necked sauropods also had long tails which helped to balance them. Can you imagine just how much this giant would have to eat each day to get its fill?

Andesaurus was named after the Andes Mountains where it was discovered.

Large sauropods like Andesaurus had little defense other than their size. Probably they stayed together in groups as a way of protecting themselves from the vicious predators that hunted them.

The most important thing about this discovery, is that the dinosaur seems to be a primitive representative of Titanosaurid sauropods, which dominated the southern continents during the Cretaceous. Just before the "Great Extinction", these animals started to invade North America.

Dino Data

Name	**Andesaurus**
Name means	**Andes lizard**
Year described	**1991**
Food	**plants**
Family	**Andesaurinae**
Lived	**Early to Late Cretaceous**
Fossils	**Argentina**
Length	**19 meters (60 feet)**
Weight	**10 – 15 metric tons (22,000 – 33,000 pounds)**

Sunset falls swiftly over the mountains as Andesaurus moves cautiously toward the high trees. It is time to feed again.

Sinraptor
The Chinese Thief

In 1987 the team members of the Canada-China Dinosaur project team toiled under the hot desert sun of northwestern China. These dino detectives had suspected for sometime that large killer theropods must have lived in the area. Clues were found everywhere. Spent teeth of large meat-eating dinosaurs were found mixed with the skeletons of the very large plant-eaters. Clearly something was killing and eating them, but what was it?

It was a tough case to solve. Suddenly, toe bones were spotted sticking out of the side of a cliff. Slowly, carefully, the scientists dug out the bones. It was an almost complete skeleton of the huge meat-eater, Sinraptor.

The mystery was solved. The long, knifelike teeth belonged to the killer Sinraptor, a major enemy of the sauropods.

Dinosaurs like Sinraptor never had to worry about losing or wearing out their teeth. As one tooth became loose and fell out, another grew in its place.

This is why the teeth of Sinraptor were found mixed in with the bones of plant-eaters. Some of its teeth had fallen out when it was eating the tasty sauropod for dinner.

Dino Data

Name	Sinraptor
Name means	Chinese thief
Year described	1993
Food	meat
Family	Sinraptoridae (Theropoda)
Lived	Late Jurassic
Fossils	Xinjiang, China
Length	7 meters (22 feet)
Weight	3 metric tons (6,600 pounds)

A baby Bellusaurus had wandered from the herd. The deadly predator Sinraptor, was smart, quick and deadly. It would soon feast. No escape would be possible for this ill-fated young one.

Einiosaurus
The Dinosaur with a Bottle Opener Nose!

If dinosaurs had parties, then Einiosaurus would have been very popular. The horn on its nose curved forward and down, just like a bottle opener. But Einiosaurus was one bottle opener you would not find in a kitchen drawer.

To begin with, Einiosaurus weighed as much as a gravel truck and was as long as a medium-sized car. To use its nose you would need to have one huge bottle that needed opening.

Scientists are not sure how Einiosaurus used its curved horn. Paleontologists believe it was only present in adults, so it is possible it was used mainly as a means of identification. Sort of like an advertisement designed to attract other individuals of the same species but of the opposite sex. Teenaged Einiosaurus horns were long and relatively straight like those of other ceratopsians.

Einiosaurus had no horns over its eyes, but at the back of its head frill were a pair of backward projecting spikes.

Many Einiosaurus were unearthed in northern Montana bone beds. This suggests that a great number of plant-eaters may have died at one time. Did an earthquake, meteorite, volcano eruption or a flood cause all these creatures to die at the same time? No one knows for sure.

Einiosaurus lived 65 million years ago, during the Late Cretaceous, just before dinosaurs disappeared from the earth.

Dino Data

Name	Einiosaurus
Named after	Blackfoot Indian word *Eini*, meaning "bison"
Year described	1995
Food	Plants
Family	Ceratopsidae
Lived	Late Cretaceous
Fossils	Montana, USA
Length	6 meters (19.5 feet)
Weight	3 metric tons (6,600 pounds)

In the heat of the afternoon, Einiosaurus rests quietly in the river. Plants to dine on are within easy reach, and the water will cool its huge body.

Utahraptor
The Cretaceous Kick Boxer

Utahraptor was so vicious it is hard to imagine who its enemies would have been other than other Utahraptors. It was one mean dinosaur judging from its teeth and claws. Definately a plant-eater's bad dream come true!

Like its relatives Deinonychus and Velociraptor, Utahraptor disemboweled its prey with a huge, sickle-shaped claw on one of its toes. This claw was normally held high off the ground so it could be kept as sharp and as dangerous as possible.

Although the Utahraptor's teeth were sharp and jagged, they were probably useful only for slicing through meat and would not have been much good for killing its prey. The hands and feet were used for that purpose.

Utahraptor was twice as big as the other "raptors" such as Velociraptor. Utahraptor was fast and smart. It may have hunted in packs like the wolves of today.

The "raptors" were some of the most birdlike of the dinosaurs. They had arms as long as those of the earliest birds and their hips are indistinguishable from those of some birds. These and other features have led some scientists to conclude that these creatures might actually be meat-eating birds rather than meat-eating dinosaurs!

Baby raptors came from eggs, but it is not known yet if the mother raptors looked after their babies.

Dino Data

Name	Utahraptor
Name means	Thief from Utah
Year described	1993
Food	meat
Family	Dromaeosauridae (Theropoda)
Lived	Early Cretaceous
Fossils	Utah, USA
Length	7 meters (24 feet)
Weight	500 kilograms (1,100 pounds)

A Mymoorapelta comes under vicious attack from a hungry Utahraptor. Mymoorapelta's sharp body prongs and tail spines may have protected it from many predators, but they definitely won't save it from the likes of Utahraptor!

Timimus

The bush fire that raged across prehistoric Australia caught Timimus in a desperate situation. Was escape possible? It was not.

Thousands of years later, the bones of Timimus were discovered and some may have been the unfortunate creatures caught in these fires. Timimus lived during the Early Cretaceous, about 100 million years ago. It was discovered by a husband and wife team of palaeontologists, who named this dinosaur after their son Tim.

This specimen discovered in 1991 is one of the few dinosaur skeletons found from "down under". Dinosaur fossils are rare in Australia and less than a dozen have been detected to date.

Timimus was discovered in an area that was considered to be cold in winter months during the time they lived. Australia at one time was much closer to the Antarctic than it is today but dinosaurs survived in these cooler climates. In contrast with other North American polar dinosaurs that could migrate to warmer places in the winter, the Australian polar dinosaurs were cut off from warmer latitudes by a sea that they could not cross.

Timimus is the first ostrich-like meat-eating dinosaur found in Australia and the only one found in this polar region. Timimus was small, a little shorter than a Volkswagon Beetle. Its long legs and ability to move fast may have protected it from its enemies. Timimus was illustrated on one of Australia's postage stamps in 1993.

Dino Data

Name	Timimus
Named after	Named after Tim
Year described	1993
Food	Meat
Family	?
Lived	Early Cretaceous
Fossils	Australia
Length	3.5 – 4.5 meters (10 –13 feet)
Weight	?

14

A raging bush fire in prehistoric Australia traps a pair of Timimus. Escape will not be possible.

Pelecanimimus
A Spanish Riddle

Pelecanimimus was a human-sized meat-eating dinosaur with a beak full of teeth—two hundred in all!

It was a theropod, which means it walked on its hind legs. How would you like to have one of these creatures tap you on the shoulder? It was tall enough to do just that!

Pelecanimimus was discovered in a 120-million-year-old lake deposit in the deserts of central Spain. Well-preserved skeletons of some of the earliest birds also have been found at this remarkable site.

Pelecanimimus was not your everyday meat-eater and may have been related to the ostrich mimicking dinosaurs, which are believed to be an evolutionary link between meat-eating dinosaurs and birds. Dino detectives think that the birdlike dinosaurs became toothless as teeth became smaller. As teeth became smaller, there were also more of them, like the Pelecanimimus who had a beak full of them.

Pelecanimimus was an important find partly because fossilized patches of skin and muscle tissue were discovered. After looking really hard, scientists found a part of the skull in a block of limestone that had been moved by a bulldozer. Spanish scientists will visit the site one more time because they think the rest of the skull is still there.

Pelecanimimus lived in the Early Cretaceous period. During this time, more varieties of dinosaurs roamed the earth than ever before.

Dino Data

Name	Pelecanimimus
Means	pelican mimic
Year described	1994
Food	meat
Family	Theropoda
Lived	Early Cretaceous
Fossils	Cuenca, Spain
Length	3 meters (10 feet)
Weight	150 – 250 kilograms (330 – 550 pounds)

Stalking through the high grass, Pelecanimimus prepares to make a snack of a large dragonfly.

Achelousaurus
The Hornless Horned Dinosaur

Maybe it used its lost horn as a stick to roast marshmallows on, and forgot to take it back home when it was done.

Achelousaurus did not have horns over its eyes either. And if Achelousaurus got together with its close relatives, Centrosaurus, and Styracosaurus, it would have been the only one that did not have a large horn on its nose.

It is possible that the bone base on Achelousaurus's head was used like a battering ram when it defended itself against carnivores. But more likely it was the base for a horn that never developed. The sturdy base was made of keratin, the same material that birds' beaks, cows' horns, mammal hair, bird feathers and even our fingernails are made from. Keratin is lighter and tougher than bone.

Achelousaurus was a plant-eater found in Montana, USA. It lived in the Late Cretaceous period when shallow seas covered much of North America. Achelousaurus weighed as much as a medium-sized delivery truck and was a little shorter than a Hummer.

Achelousaurus was named after the Greek river god, Achelous. Achelous took the form of a bull to fight Hercules, but lost when one of his horns was cut off.

Dino Data

Name	Achelousaurus
Name means	Achelous of Greek mythology
Year described	1995
Food	plants
Family	Ceratopsidae
Lived	Late Cretaceous
Fossils	Montana, USA
Length	6 meters (20 feet)
Weight	3 metric tons (6,600 pounds)

18

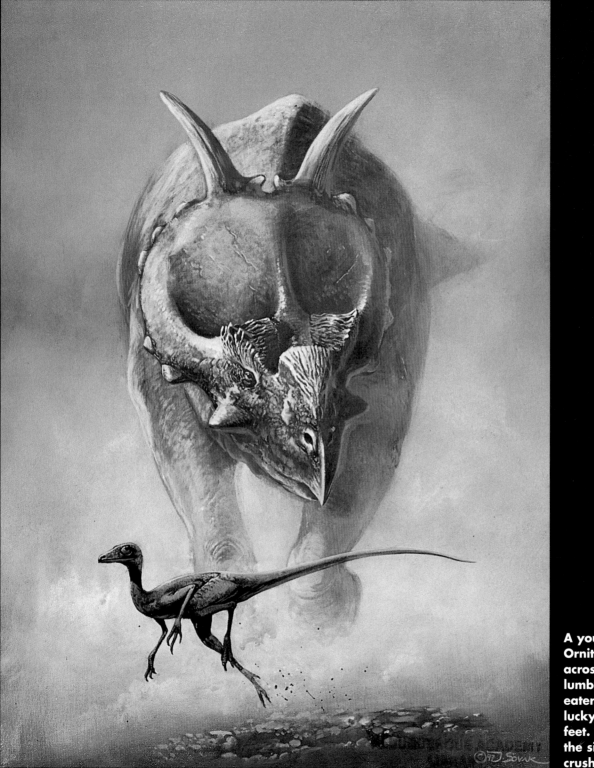

A young turkey-sized Ornithomimus sprints across the path of a lumbering giant plant-eater. Ornithomimus is lucky he's so fast on his feet. The Achelousaurus is the size of truck and could crush him in an instant!

Seismosaurus
The Longest Dinosaur Yet!

It's a shaker, it's a quaker. The longest dinosaur found to date is called the "earthquake dinosaur."

Seismosaurus was longer than the blue whale, which is the largest animal on the earth today. If you can imagine a giant dinosaur that was longer than five school buses in a row, then you know the approximate size of an adult Seismosaurus.

Seismosaurus, like all sauropods, was a plant-eater. Although it is the longest animal known to date, its legs were shorter than closely related animals like Diplodocus.

Because of this close relationship to Diplodocus, Seismosaurus probably had long, pencil-like teeth. Its mouth was small and the teeth were too simple to chew the leaves that it combed from the trees. So Seismosaurus swallowed stones to grind up the leaves in its stomach and make them easier to digest. Many species of birds today use the same system since they lack teeth to grind up seeds and other plant matter.

Computer modeling has recently shown that the tails of Seismosaurus and its kin were capable of moving faster than the speed of sound! In this way their tails acted like bullwhips, which could produce loud, terrifying noises as they broke the sound barrier.

The noise created by their tails may have not only kept predators at bay, but also may have been used to communicate with other sauropods.

Dino Data

Name	Seismosaurus halli
Name means	earthquake lizard
Year described	1991
Food	plants
Family	Sauropod
Lived	Late Jurassic
Fossils	New Mexico, USA
Length	45 meters (150 feet)
Weight	40 metric tons (88,000 pounds)

The earth probably shook as this monster moved slowly along the edge of the forest. Food was close at hand, and the huge meat-eating predators that stalked it were easier to spot.

Gasparinisaura
A Tiny, Rare Dinosaur

Gasparinisaura is a rare find because it was small. In the world of dinosaurs, where giants ruled, it was only about the size of a medium-sized dog. Gasparinisaura was very small indeed!

The bones of small dinosaurs are hardly ever found. The reason is that large meat-eating dinosaurs would probably eat the very small dinosaurs, bones, flesh, skin and all. Gasparinisaura was just a between-meal snack!

The other reason Gasparinisaura is rare and unusual is because it was the odd one out, even when it was alive. This happened because Gasparinisaura was an Iguanodont (a plant-eating dinosaur) that lived in an area heavily populated by larger plant-eaters called hadrosaurs (also known as duck-billed dinosaurs). Eventually, the small Gasparinisaura disappeared and were replaced by their bigger cousins.

If the larger meat-eaters were sloppy enough to let any Gasparinisaura bones fall from their jaws, scavengers were ready to pick the bones clean. Any bones left after all that fell apart and were scattered. But some Gasparinisaura didn't die in the jaws of a theropod, and they left their bones to fossilize and be found by dino detectives millions of years later.

Gasparinisaura probably stayed around longer than other Iguanadonts because it had long, strong legs and could escape its enemies. Other creatures that lived in the same environment with these dinosuars were turtles, crocodiles, theropods, sauropods and fish.

Dino Data

Name	**Gasparinisaura**
Named after	Z. Gasparini, its discoverer
Year Described	1996
Food	Plants
Family	Iguanodont
Lived	Late Cretaceous
Fossils	Argentina
Length	70 centimeters (2.5 feet)
Weight	10 kilograms (22 pounds)

Run for your life! Forget the eggs! Time to exit this scene! One Gasparinisaura is already caught in the deadly jaws of Abelisaurus as its two companions make a run for their lives.

Argentinosaurus
Heaviest of all dinosaurs

The heavy weight champion of the dinosaur world was Argentinosaurus!

The heaviest dinosaur discovered to date, it may have been only half the length of Seismosaurus but it was big and bulky and more than double the weight.

It is hard to imagine how such a massive animal could have acquired enough food to reach that size. Can you picture how many hundreds of kilos of tree leaves, plants and nuts this monster must have eaten each day to satisfy its hunger?

In Argentina, paleontologists (the name for people who search for dinosaurs) found the remains of this very, very large sauropod. They were amazed by the size of its bones. A single piece of backbone was nearly to the height of a small adult human.

Argentinosaurus probably had few enemies except for the huge carnivores that lived in the same area and hunted them. In 1997 an expedition discovered a fossil site where many meat-eaters related to Giganotosaurus had died. Perhaps they were traveling in a group so they could capture giant sauropods like Argentinosaurus.

During prehistoric times, creatures other than dinosaurs also grew to enormous sizes. Crocodiles 12 meters (40 feet) long were just one group of large neighbors of the dinosaurs.

Dino Data

Name	Argentinosaurus
Means	Argentine lizard
Year described	1993
Food	plants
Family	Titanosauridae (Sauropoda)
Lived	Late Jurassic
Fossils	Neuquen, Argentina, South America.
Length	28 meters (90 feet)
Weight	100 metric tons (220,400 pounds)

Three Xenotarsosaurus predators encircle a huge plant-eater caught too far away from its herd. These carnivores will need all the help they can get to bring this giant down.

Cryolophosaurus
The Frozen Dinosaur nicknamed Elvisaurus

Cryolophosaurus did not get its name because it cried a lot. But as the biggest meat-eater of Early Jurassic times, it probably made other dinosaurs cry. It was about half as long as a city bus and weighed as much as a small delivery truck.

Cryolophosaurus's name comes from the word *frozen*. The fossil bones of the creature were discovered by paleontologists who were surprised to find bones just 360 kilometers (200 miles) from the South Pole.

The front of the skull and part of the skeleton had been ground away by a recent glacier, but the back half of the skull and much of the skeleton was recovered. Scientists had to work in difficult conditions with sub-zero temperatures, hard rock and inadequate tools. More of the skeleton may be in the rocks, but another expedition will not be launched until 1999.

The most unusual feature of Cryolophosaurus is the crest on the top of its head. Unlike most crested theropods, Cryolophosaurus's crest does not run along the length of the skull, but lies across the top.

To some people the crest looks like an snow shovel, but to others it looks like an Elvis Presley style "jelly roll" hairdo, which is why some jokingly refer to this dinosaur as Elvisaurus. Since this discovery was made in the Antarctic, this discovery made this dinosaur a "cool dude", just like Elvis.

Cryolophosaurus probably had no natural enemies although the bones seem to have been scavenged by small theropods before they were buried. The skeleton of a prosauropod dinosaur was found with Cryolophosaurus and may have been its last meal.

Dino Data

Name	Cryolophosaurus
Name means	frozen crested lizard
Year described	1994
Food	meat
Family	Abelisauridae (Theropoda)
Lived	Early Jurassic
Fossils	Antarctica
Length	6.5 meters (21 feet)
Weight	2.5 metric tons (5,500 pounds)

Cryolophosaurus is badly hurt after falling from the cliff above. Small carnivores, who are no match for a healthy Cryolophosaurus, now wait patiently for it to die.

Afrovenator

If you find a hundred dollars on the ground, then you can imagine how excited scientists were when the bones of a new dinosaur called Afrovenator were found. What made this discovery even more exciting is that the dino detectives were actually searching for fossil fish and ended up with a dinosaur!

With such good luck, they went back to search for more fossils and found huge plant-eating dinosaurs that were dinner for the predator Afrovenator.

Afrovenator was found in the region we know today as the Sahara Desert, but in prehistoric times this area featured abundant plant life that supported giant plant-eaters. Huge trees and other plants were easy food for the giant sauropods, and as luck will have it, home to the huge predators that stalked them. Fish, turtles and crocodiles were also neighbors of these creatures.

Cautiously watching the movements of the predator is Trionyx, a three-clawed, common soft-shelled fresh water turtle. Its diet was fish and insects and it did not want to become a diet snack for Afrovenator.

Some scientists believe Afrovenator was skilled enough to kill large plant-eaters twice its size. This fierce hunter was a bit longer than a city bus. Its powerful jaws and curved claws on its forelimbs were used to grab and hold the victim in a death grip. The rest is history!

Dino Data

Name	Afrovenator
Name means	African hunter
Year described	1994
Food	meat
Family	Saurischia
Lived	Late Jurassic
Fossils	Africa
Length	9 meters (30 feet)
Weight	2 metric tons (4,400 pounds)

Afrovenator, the long-legged swift hunter moves quietly through the forest, always alert for any careless plant-eater that will become its next meal.

Giganotosaurus
A Sauropod's Worst Nightmare!

Giganotosaurus probably had no enemies, but every other dinosaur that lived in South America 100 million years ago was definitely on the menu for this giant meat-eater. This bulky beast lived about 30 million years before Tyrannosaurus rex became known as the king of the carnivores.

In its time Giganotosaurus was the unchallenged emperor. It was at least as long as Tyrannosaurus rex and considerably heavier. Giganotosaurus may have been the biggest meat-eating animal that ever walked the earth.

The skull and upper leg bones of Giganotosaurus are larger than those of Tyrannosaurus rex, but its teeth are only half the size. Their narrow, knifelike appearance suggests that they were used differently than the bone-crushing teeth of Tyrannosaurus rex.

Giganotosaurus's teeth were perfect, however, for biting large chunks of hide and muscle from the flanks of some unlucky sauropod. The teeth are so sharklike that the family Giganotosaurus belongs to is called the Carcharodontosauridae, meaning "Carcharodon lizard." Carcharodon is the scientific name for the great white shark.

Giganotosaurus lived during the Late Cretaceous period, the time just before dinosaurs became extinct. Millions of years later an amateur fossil hunter discovered its bones while fossil hunting in the badlands of Argentina.

Dino Data

Name	**Giganotosaurus**
Name means	**Giant southern lizard**
Year described	**1995**
Food	**meat**
Family	**Carcharodontosauridae (Theropoda)**
Lived	**Late Cretaceous**
Fossils	**Neuquen, Argentina**
Length	**12 meters (40 feet)**
Weight	**6 metric tons (13,000 pounds)**

The predator Carnotaurus, that looks like a bulldog with horns, has its dinner interrupted by a much larger meat-eating cousin. Giganotosaurus will dine well today, but Carnotaurus will have to kill again to keep from going hungry.

Index

Glossary

Abelisaurus - a large carnivore

Bellusaurus - plant-eater

Carnosaurus - meat-eater

Edmarka - a carnivore described in 1992

Ornithomimus -ostrich-like dinosaur

Mymoorapelta - new armored dinosaur (1994)

Text copyright © 1998
Philip J. Currie and Colleayn O. Mastin
Illustration copyright © 1998 Jan Sovak

Canadian Cataloguing in Publication Data
Currie, Philip, J. 1949– Newest and coolest dinosaurs
Includes index. ISBN 1-895910-41-2 (bound)
1. Dinosaurs—Juvenile literature,
I. Mastin, Colleayn O. (Colleayn Olive).
II. Sovak, Jan, 1952– III. Title.
QE862.D5C877 1998   j567.9'1   C96-910710-2

Printed in Canada
Designed By Boldface Technologies Inc.

To the ones that helped, thank you:
Emelee Marchant, Kelly Dinney, Kelly Meston, Michelle Locken and families.

This book is dedicated to Dan Holden and Paul-Herman Burgel.

6 5 4 3 2